IT'S TIME *to* START LIVING

—— *with* ——

PASSION!

YOUR JOURNEY
To Self-Discovery

JEAN PAUL PAULYNICE, MBA

PAULYNICE CONSULTING GROUP
Your Success Is Our Business!

Published by Paulynice Consulting Group, LLC

ISBN: 978-1-7330427-9-6 (Hardback)
ISBN: 978-1-7335601-9-1 (Paperback)
ISBN: 978-1-7330427-0-3 (eBook)
ISBN: 978-1-7335601-2-2 (Audiobook)

Printed in the United States of America.

CONTENTS

PART ONE: MY STORY

PART TWO: YOUR WORKBOOK

*DEDICATED TO
EVERYONE WORKING
TO FIND THEIR PURPOSE
AND FOLLOW THEIR
PASSION AND BLISS.*

*MAY YOU LIVE WITH
COURAGE ALWAYS!*

ACKNOWLEDGMENT

I want to thank my loving and supportive wife, Bency, and my two beautiful daughters, Saïdah and Elyse, who provide unending inspiration. This book is for you. For all your many talents and the endless love and laughter we share. It's when I'm with you that I am blissful.

I also dedicate this to my grandfather, Andre, who raised and shaped me to become the successful man I am today and whose eternal love and guidance are with me in whatever I pursue. Grandpa Andre, you are my ultimate role model.

PREFACE

A couple of years ago, I was working so hard I forgot about my friends, family, and health. I was growing my career, working in some of the best organizations. I was blessed with all of the opportunities that I dreamt about. Each day, I was chasing some new goal and new illusion. I thought that every new job would bring me contentment. I felt I would find something that resonated with me. I thought, at some point, I'd find happiness in what I was doing.

But the reality was, I was not happy. I was, in fact, miserable.

I knew I needed a reboot. I needed something fresh to keep me going because I couldn't continue doing what I was doing. While my corporate job gave me immense experience, it had taken away my creativity and freedom. I felt empty. It was not clear what I wanted to do the next day, or even the next month or year. I was staring into an abyss.

Why was I working so hard? Was it for the money? Was it for some fulfillment? Honestly, most days, I felt as if I was chasing money and running after bills. Ultimately, I didn't want to get out of bed and go to my nine-to-five job.

That was my turning point.

I needed to do more with my life. I think most people feel this way. I needed something that excited me. I needed some fire in my soul. I wanted to find something that would give me gusto – something that I would be excited to do every day, even without pay. I needed work that didn't feel like work.

I wanted to do something I loved, that would give me more time with my family. Something that would allow me to create real connections with friends, leave me with more time for self-care, and impact people the best way I knew how.

Let me ask you something. *If you could do one thing to transform your life, what would it be?* If you're not sure, this book will help you find some starting points to move forward and some insights into your situation.

I am Jean Paul Paulynice. This book is a record of my journey to find more passion and purpose in my life. It describes both the good and bad experiences and the losses and the victories. I hope it inspires you to move out of your comfort zone and ignites your passion, purpose, and bliss in life.

CHAPTER ONE

WHO AM I? WHY AM I HERE?

Finding my passion has been a journey of life itself. As long as I can remember, I have tried to figure out what my passion is, often having to pay a high price along the way. I have sacrificed opportunities for high-paying jobs and free time for myself to relax in pursuit of a more invigorating life. From attempting different careers to pursuing different lifestyles, I have tried everything I could to discover my passions. Unfortunately, I have had to experience the burden of trying out things that I did not like in life, though in time I came to see this burden as a luxury—that I had time to experience so many different things and had the freedom to explore. I think that this is something that we often take for granted—the amount of choice that we do have in the modern world. Sometimes it can feel like trying out new things to discover that they don't work is a waste of time. I have come to realize that what felt like setbacks or wastes of time were important learning experiences on my journey. Surprisingly, even to this day, I am still searching for more things that excite me to the core. I have discovered truths about what makes me happy, what makes me feel alive, but I am still in pursuit of a better, more fulfilling life and a better me, and this is somewhere I will always be.

These goals may sound all too familiar to you: the process of starting over and over again in search of what you want. You may have read other books on the subject and are still stuck. For some of you, this process has involved changing careers, changing friends, beliefs, or lifestyles. Some of you may have woken up one morning and decided to move to a new place to find your passion. Some of you may not be at this point yet. These are huge changes, but the good thing is that it is not as elusive as it may seem if you persevere.

What makes you think you have found your life passion? How do you know that you have reached your purpose? Is it your finances? Is it when you get the promotion you have wanted?

First of all, passion in life is not something that comes to you. You don't just wake up one day and hear your life passion call out, "*Hey, pal, you have found me.*" No, that is not the way passion is discovered.

It's your job and your duty to find your passion in life. It is a journey, sometimes a difficult process. *What is it that passionately motivates you? What could you do for years without getting bored? What could you do for the rest of your life without the reward of payment?* If you had the total financial freedom to choose anything, *what would it be?* That right there, could be your passion.

The sensation that comes with it, when you do find true passion, is surreal. You automatically know that *"this is it!"*

WHAT LIGHTS YOU UP?

When you find your passion, you'll experience peace and satisfaction. It is as if you are entering an entirely new world and chapter in your life. You can see the possibilities and the impact before you even begin. It will get your blood racing.

A perfect example would be a day at an exciting job. After you have worked on a project, you come outside, and you see the world differently — the joy that you have is almost indescribable. The gut feeling that you get is just different. You start seeing life through different lenses, and your perspective in life is beautiful and pristine. You don't feel the resentment that comes from working in a place or on a project in which you find no enjoyment.

It's like a brand-new day. Everything is distinctly different. The gloom, the sadness, and the boredom have all gone away. You wake up and smile because you are happy and eager to try different things.

You are eager and confident to try exciting challenges. The sensation, the feeling, the vision, the way you see things is completely changed.

You are happy, and when you approach people, your environment and energy changes. It's like you have been elevated to a higher level.

Passion for life is more than just a job, positive relationships, or fulfilling hobbies; it is a mindset, and it is the result of tenacity and grit. Passion for life comes from following your bliss, despite the setbacks or challenges. If you follow your passion, you will reap the rewards. If you settle for mediocrity, you will pay the price. Many people find their passion when they know that their actions can change the world. *What talents do you possess that you can give to others, or what skills can you develop?*

To find life passion, we all have to experience things we like and don't like, but we suffer if we don't follow what motivates us. Until you find your life passion, your life is always a struggle; sometimes you find yourself wondering, *"Am I supposed to be alive? What is my purpose?"*

On the other hand, when you do find your life passion, your perspective changes. You make the daily decision to take part in something you enjoy. Today you can make a difference in another person's life. Today is the day to change things. Life passion, from my perspective, is seeing the beauty in things and living through it.

One fall day, I was driving through a back road to pick up my daughter, Saïdah, from kindergarten. I was struck in awe when I took a moment to see the beauty of the changing leaves in that crisp fall afternoon. I have certainly experienced many fall seasons before, but in that moment, it felt more spectacular to me. With life passion by your side, you can take a moment to reflect on the flowers, the trees, and the leaves.

Imagine driving through the same backroad without life passion by your side; you are, like, "*How annoying! Why are these leaves falling? They are obstructing my view. They are making a mess of everything. I'm going to have to spend so much time raking leaves this weekend at home!*" Life passion is life itself. It is the price and the reward. It is what life is all about. Regardless of the circumstances, you must find what makes you happy, work on it, and believe that you can change the world.

CHAPTER TWO

UNDERSTANDING MYSELF

So how and when did I know that I had found my passion in life?

Let's start by learning what life passion is not. I have gone through a few experiences and jobs to know what exactly life passion is and what it is not.

There are things that I have done that I outrightly felt were not my passion. I could not imagine waking up to the same thing the next day.

MY EXPERIENCE WORKING IN THE LABORATORY

After graduation, my first corporate job involved working in the biotech field, specifically working in a lab. I put on a white lab coat every day and was required to be in a gown when the procedures involved sterilized products or chemicals.

In the lab, I spent hours doing experiments in this bulky and uncomfortable clothing. Sometimes it felt like I could barely breathe, and it was incredibly lonely. It's just you, the products, the chemicals, and the experiments. If you tried to sneeze, you would probably knock something down. To me, that kind of environment was very restrictive. I felt stuck, like a sterilized chemical itself. It was an isolating and suffocating routine.

While this was not my way of doing things, was it possible that it could be a passion for someone else? Yes, it could be. So, finding a passion is a personal journey. It is as personal as your interests and preferences. When you have found your passion, you will feel it.

While this experience was a negative one for me, it helped me to learn what I *don't* want to do. The negative emotions that I experienced, as a result, pushed me to try something else.

MY EXPERIENCE AS A STAY-AT-HOME DAD

I love my children. I am always looking for ways to squeeze more time with them into my schedule. The memories that I make with my children are invaluable. At one point, I thought that if I could have the opportunity to take care of them all day, it would be so fulfilling and finally, I could shape them into the ideal humans of which I have always dreamt.

I decided to give it a try. The first day was tough, but I comforted myself, saying that things are obviously harder on the first day and I'd get the hang of it eventually. The stress that came with it left me wondering how a stay-at-home parent finds balance in life. Changing diapers, preparing food, cleaning the house, doing laundry, ensuring that they eat well and on time, and the bedtime routine got the better of me.

Most of the time, I found myself giving the children convenient prepared food so I could avoid cooking. My logic seemed to work for them since I didn't have to scream myself hoarse to make them eat. I found that being an authority figure in this way in the household did not come naturally for me. It didn't take long before I could see that I was setting myself and the children on a path of unhealthy eating.

If I were to continue, I could imagine everyone in my household, including the kids, gaining at least ten pounds per week. They would be eating high-calorie, low-nutrient processed foods, sitting in front of the TV, barely moving all day.

Imagine the resentment and feeling of hopelessness that would come with this kind of a scenario three or four months down the line. I honestly applaud and acknowledge the parents who do this day in and day out. The sacrifices they make every single second are so immense. I felt depressed and sad that my natural temperament did not align with this lifestyle. I love my children, and I love spending time with them, but staying home all day made me feel stuck in a rut. Eventually, I decided that my children would be happier if their day-to-day living activities were managed by someone who had more aptitude for childcare—someone who did this type of work because they were passionate about it. I knew that they would be more receptive to a different style of boundary setting and redirection, and I couldn't force myself to be someone that I wasn't for the sake of their development. I knew that I would have a happier family if I were happy. I decided to pursue other work, and my family was better for it, revealing a learning experience for me, and it taught me a lot about myself and my role as a father.

Even if something is good, noble, and worth investing in, it does not mean that it is your passion in life. Something you need to know at this point, as you are seeking to find your passion, is that passion is narrow.

Passion is not about being everywhere and doing everything.

It is about something with which you individually connect. You can do it with grace and for long hours. You can go on and on because you find the motivation within you. You cannot be good at all things, but you can be good at one thing that you love. That is your purpose.

CHAPTER THREE

THE EYE OPENER

After working in the lab for several years, I went on to further my education, which was very exciting for me. I enjoyed going back to school to get my MBA in Finance and Management Information Systems. I saw how I could apply data analytics in different areas. That's what I enjoyed.

My first practical experience in the field after graduate school was working for a health insurance firm, which meant I would be using Microsoft Excel almost every day, as it was the trend in the finance world. And I was proficient in it.

I was grateful to the Almighty God that I had gained good skills, and I could finally apply those skills and experiences in everything I do. Even at that point, I didn't see myself using Excel every day. The mundane tasks included making sure data was accurate and making sure my code worked well, especially when doing the coding using SQL. When you get requirements from clients, you need to ensure you interpret them correctly.

The thought of sitting behind the computer and capturing all the data correctly every single day wasn't unpleasant, but I knew it was not what I wanted to do for the rest of my life, spending eight hours a day behind the computer and only talking to the screen and programming. I wasn't completely satisfied in work that was devoid of human interaction. I needed to find something where I was interacting with other human beings more frequently and where I could move around more often. More than that, I needed something a little more dynamic and exciting.

Let us reflect on my last experience. *Is it possible that you could find something that you enjoy doing, but it's still not it?* When I was in school, working towards receiving my MBA, I knew I had finally found one link that had been missing. I already knew I loved working with numbers, so I thought I had finally found something with which I could connect. It did not take long for me to realize that Excel and lab work were not my passions. Yes, presently, I enjoy dealing with numbers, verifying data, and ensuring I give the clients the correct output, but it is not my entire being.

Being happy in the moment is important. You may want to stick to what you are doing just because it makes you happy now, or because you feel comfortable doing it, but if it doesn't align to your dreams and purpose, the happiness will be temporary.

I knew if I continued crunching numbers without finding any meaning in what I was doing, the misery would return, and my lack of fulfillment would show. The stress and dissatisfaction would spill over to my relationships with family and friends. To protect myself and those around me, I knew I had to act. I had to align my dreams with the work I was doing.

If you are doing something that you enjoy right now but are not sure if it is your passion, don't be discouraged. It is vital that you go through the processes and experiences to help you bring out the real you. Think about it this way: exposure to different environments and experiences tests your character, ability, and values. These are the three ingredients that will lead you to your passion.

If I had not interacted with clients after receiving my MBA, I would not have known that I'd find a lot of satisfaction in helping people. It is this process that gave me a glimpse into how it feels to help people make the right decisions and grow.

In a nutshell, allow yourself to go through the process, the experiences, the disappointments, and the mistakes. I doubt that there is anyone in the world who landed on their passion on the first attempt. Even those who did had to go through a series of disappointments to test if this was meant for them and if they had the grit to defend their passion.

You will be shaken, and there will be barriers. You are allowed to make mistakes before you land on the real thing. One thing is for sure: once you find your passion, you will feel it, you will see it, and you will know it.

CHAPTER FOUR

MY PASSIONS

One might ask, what is my passion, then? If I don't find fulfillment from any of this stuff I tried, even activities that I am pretty good at and have identified as things that I like, then what is my passion?

Over the years, I have found that I have many passions; no single thing on its own is enough to fulfill me, and I am continually searching for more ways to infuse my life with bliss. I have found that, when I am living my life with passion, I am maintaining those areas of life that excite me, and I am challenging myself to develop more areas of life to explore.

One of my most significant sources of happiness is spending quality time with my family. I couldn't be any happier when I am with them. It's thrilling and exciting to watch my beautiful family growing with me. I enjoy spending time with my incredible wife and amazing daughters to strengthen the bonds of our household. As a stay-at-home dad, I felt stressed, and it was incredibly tough since it wasn't the role with which I was most passionate. Spending quality time with my family is more enjoyable than assuming the role of a stay-at-home parent. For instance, I was able to develop a more meaningful bond with my children when we went for a stroll at the park, visited the museum, or read a book in our backyard as a family, instead of worrying about completing chores day in and day out with no end in sight. We truly feel blessed as a family, and I am grateful for the many blessings that the Almighty God has bestowed upon us.

My second passion is running and especially running outside in nature. I can walk or run outside for a long time. I have no problem doing it over and over with no boredom whatsoever. Cardiovascular exercise makes me feel livelier. When I feel energetic, I can find more joy in everyday things.

My third passion is lifting weights, and I enjoy it. I also feel satisfaction and an increase in self-esteem that comes with my appearance after a strong and long workout.

I am an avid swimmer and like to push my limits in the water. The constant resistance of the water against my muscles tones them and makes me feel strong. Feeling good about the body you're in helps you to feel good about your interactions with other people and gives you confidence. If you know that you can accomplish feats of strength or endurance, it reminds you that you can overcome other challenges, like developing your mind if you go back to school, or challenging yourself to become a better public speaker so you can get your dream job.

There is a special feeling you get when people are telling you how great or healthy you look; it's the same as when you are praised at work for a job well done, or when you did well on a paper in school. It feels even greater if you have worked for it while enjoying the process. Self-actualization in your body, as well as your mind, is of the utmost importance when it comes to living a life of passion and bliss.

My fourth passion is technology. I like building websites, branding, and putting creativity into what I am doing as a consultant. I like to see progress. I like to see growth, bringing pieces together, and building a dream. *"How can I make somebody happy?"* I always ask myself.

When you create a website, it's not like when you're programming. Building a website is more creative. You put in design elements and see your clients enjoy what you have created, and this feels fantastic. They see the work you put into their projects; they see the progress. Furthermore, the more clients you have, the more you expand on your creativity.

As an entrepreneur, each client brings a new need to the table, a new challenge; however, it is not like working for a corporation. After you leave your position at the corporation, your identity is no longer connected to their organization. You are just another person that used to work for them. But if you do fantastic work for a client, you build a personal connection. You can always use that work for your portfolio, and you can always reflect on the progress, transformation, the things in which you excel. Again, there is an impact on the client, and it is visible. You are no longer hidden behind a corporate wall.

In technology, I found a field of study in which I am passionate. In working with clients, I found a work style that suits my personality and my values. I encourage you to find subjects that excite you and try out different ways of working, whether it be traditional employment, contract work, or entrepreneurship. Maybe it makes you feel vibrant if you work a more physical job even if that's not what society is telling you to do. Listen to your body, listen to your instincts, and don't be afraid to try new things.

My fifth passion is landscaping. For me, landscaping is seeing how you can transform your surroundings into something amazing. You can see how green your area looks; you can see how clean it is and what you can do with it in different seasons. When you add lighting, flowers, and unique plants, this is simply nature at its best. You can modify and uplift your environment to your taste. You can create a confident mood and brighten an otherwise dull and boring surrounding to an ecstatic and luxurious feel. You can see nature from your view. It helps you to appreciate the natural world and creativity.

Your environment plays a big part in your happiness. Maybe you don't have a big yard, but you could spend time decorating, painting your house, adding personalized touches to the place where you spend so much of your time.

My sixth passion is working with people. I have found that sometimes it takes a new opinion and a little bit of push to unlock great potential. That is why I enjoy consulting one-on-one with people. It is about impact, working with clients and seeing the difference you can make, and seeing how you can help the person make more money.

For me, working is not entirely about making money; it is about helping others succeed. Often, when you work with people, you are uplifting them. When I help my clients, it transforms their lives, not just their businesses, and it becomes the best feeling for me.

Maybe part of your passion is sourced from the satisfaction that comes with helping people and helping their dreams become a reality. Is there a way that you can add more of this into your interpersonal life, into your job, into your philanthropic activities? You could help clients, children, people who are disabled, or the elderly. You could help your peers, and you can help those less fortunate. Feeling like you have something to give or contribute will boost your self-esteem.

In a world where everyone is busy trying to make it through life, we rarely get an audience to explore our ideas.

As a person that has struggled to make a breakthrough in the path of finding my passion, I like hearing about other people's experiences. I have often asked myself, *"What if I can make the process easier for them?"*

Sometimes, all we need is a thought partner or a springboard. We have great ideas, we sort of know what we want, and all that we need is a reality check. I like to consult with people so that I can help them fact check. I also find it rewarding if I can enrich or do some damage control to help someone unlock their potential, my motive to consult whenever I get a chance.

Are you wondering why I have listed all the things I love to do? Does this mean that all of the above are my passions? As I mentioned earlier, passion is a process. It involves going through several experiences to know exactly what makes you tick. Sometimes the thing that you are passionate about can be diversified into different paths – but the goal remains the same.

Understanding this will help you establish balance in your life while making use of your passions.

If I bring these activities and pursuits together, I end up getting the bigger picture of my passion in life. If you already know a series of things that make you happy; there is no point continuing to divert your energy further.

CHAPTER FIVE

YOUR BLISS IS WITHIN REACH

Bliss is absolute happiness. It is the highest degree of joy, peace, fulfillment, and purpose. Bliss enables us to create the type of life and experience that forces us to be the best versions of ourselves.

Bliss is not an object you desire. It's not a car or a house. It is not a place where you can travel. It is not a title, a job, a promotion, or a bank account. No! Bliss is a feeling and experience, not an object.

For me, bliss is the smell of fresh air while I take a long nature walk in the last quiet moments of my morning. It is the peace I find in experiencing the cool moonlit night. It is the gratitude in watching leaves fall along my path during the autumn season. It is the hypnotizing jog through a park. It is the joy I get during each precious moment with my family. Bliss is knowing that I have power and full control over my feelings, and not giving that control away to someone else. Bliss is doing the things I love all day, any day. Bliss is leaving space for renewal and rejuvenation.

BORN FOR BLISS

Imagine your state of happiness when you're doing something that brings you a deep sense of joy. It could be your passion or anything that you love doing. Running, playing the piano, or just being around your family. That kind of deep happiness is bliss. And in this state, your body, mind, and heart are in sync. You can almost listen to the voice of your heart. Everything resonates well with you.

Not to worry, the true version of yourself is within reach.

I'd like to share with you one of my favorite exercises. A powerful exercise that can help you tap into your energy and figure out the source of your deepest joys.

I'd like to share with you one of my favorite exercises. A powerful exercise that can help you tap into your energy and figure out the source of your deepest joys.

I find it best when I am closing my eyes. Only then can I fully sync my mind, body, and soul.

Now, I want us to do this together.

Think about the times you have been deeply happy. Not simply excited, not just thrilled. The moments that your happiness went beyond a smile. Can you feel the joy in your heart? The tingly feeling deep inside you? At that moment, everything else does not matter. At that moment, you're only mindful of the sensations in your body. You can let the good vibes and energy flutter in your mind.

I'd like you to document that feeling and hold it close to your heart. It will serve as your guidepost. The secret to finding your bliss is in maintaining that positivity and those happy vibes, day in and day out. How can you do that? How do you get there? It's simple!

THE FIRST STEP INVOLVES ENGAGING IN A BIT OF PROFOUND SELF-ANALYSIS

What's your life's purpose? If you are in this life, then it must be because there is a purpose. There must be a reason why you are alive today. That's for sure. So how do you get to know your purpose? How can you know your "higher calling"? You have to work for it, search for it, and nurture it.

It is not easy, but it is doable.

You have to be able to listen to yourself and have a profound dialogue. Ask yourself these questions: "*What can I do today?*"; "*What brings me deep happiness?*"; "*Where is my bliss?*"; "*How do I find my bliss?*"; and "*How can I get there?*"

To reach your bliss, that level of profound happiness, you have to go out there and try different things, test different stuff, and think about different possibilities. Along the way, you'll fall and fail. But once you hit your impetus, your life will take a whole new direction. Once you reach your bliss, your life will undoubtedly move in the direction of full self-actualization. Only then can you achieve your full potential.

Let me give another illustration of choosing happiness.

Most of us have that perfect restaurant we love frequenting. When you go to the restaurant, you'll peruse the menu looking for your special treat. You have a list of choices to make. Based on your choices, you can pick the food that you love. You can select the food that you know you will enjoy — that sumptuous dish that hits your taste buds in all the right spots.

You know that you'll not be obligated to eat it. This particular food you love will make you happy. It is going to change your day and your mood towards everything; it is going to make you feel better. And when you finally get to eat that food, you feel different, rejuvenated!

Here's another analogy.

When you're dating, you're going to meet different people. There are people you're going to meet with whom you automatically don't feel any connection. You know right away from your gut that this person is not your type. You can tell that you're not compatible.

Then, you'll meet somebody that aligns with your energy. The person's vibe is in total sync with yours. You can see that there is bliss in your experience. You can feel the sensation, *and it becomes the one. Regardless of our differences, we can work things out. We can make a difference in the world. We can live life together*. When you feel that sensation, there is deeper happiness. You'll have reached your bliss.

In these two illustrations, we make choices, either between two of your favorite dishes or between two dates. Since we want what the heart wants, we go for those things or people that make us excited. That way, we are happy. Extremely happy. We experience bliss, even if it is momentary. Apply these analogies to what you do with your time and your work. You have choices. If you choose the things that *you* want to do, it will impact your day and your life.

Your bliss is within reach. It is something that people often experience when trying new things. We have seen how, through effort and decisiveness, you can attain happiness when you're eating your favorite food or when you're dating.

Surprisingly, when it comes to everyday work, tasks, career, and long-term goals, people tend to overlook bliss. It's baffling how most people think that they have to accept life as it is, and they become accustomed to what they're doing. They don't enjoy it. They don't find bliss in what they're doing.

CHAPTER SIX

THE WALL BETWEEN YOU AND TRUE HAPPINESS

Not many people are walking around feeling blissful—or even remotely happy, for that matter. When you talk to some people about what they do, you can automatically see that there is misery in whatever they wake up every day to pursue. Today, you'll be surprised how many people are stuck in a rut: they'll pay bills, live life, wake up to the same routine, without questioning anything.

Even some of the most educated people cannot somehow move away from the "life happens" perspective. I choose to call it the "settle for anything" lifestyle. The other day, I was having a conversation with a scientist, and we were chatting about life and our long-term goals. Then, I asked him what he would be doing in the next five to ten years. His response was: *"I only have a five-year plan. I will keep doing what I am doing, and after five years, maybe I could try something else. After five years, if God wants me to, maybe I can volunteer, or try different stuff.*" He wasn't actively pursuing his interests, and his attitude came off as resigned and complacent.

I realized that we are often afraid to chase bliss. We are afraid of taking the path less traveled. We are afraid of making hard decisions. Why? Because our not-so-blissful comfort zone is cozy. It's less disruptive. It is society-friendly. It is routine. It is what it is! But isn't that limiting our true potential?

WHY DOES BLISS NEVER SEEM TO TRANSLATE INTO EVERYDAY LIFE?

Why pursue something when, in fact, you don't enjoy it? I think the main reason we do this is that we don't want to take the bull by its horns. We don't want to face our layers of inner turmoil, insecurity, and struggles. When you think that you're all set in life, and you don't want to be open-minded about other possibilities, it becomes tough to take any action.

Because in five years, or any other timetable you have set in your mind, anything could happen. You could be in the worst position, a situation so bad in which you may never get to fulfill what you planned or hoped. The job you have now may not exist. Even your fallback plan, your plan B, may not manifest.

So, if you don't start acting now, you may never truly live up to your full potential. You have to take baby steps and start asking yourself the hard questions: *What can I do? How do I find my bliss? How do I start doing the things that I enjoy?*

IS BLISS THAT ELUSIVE?

No!

I think everyone has the ability and capacity to find their bliss. The problem is, we are too caught up in everyday life and routines to break the cycle. Sometimes we are so caught up in what people think that we forget about our happiness. We are living in a bubble where social media approval has made it very hard for us to try different things. We are chasing societal validation at the expense of our bliss. We are more fearful than ever of judgment because we feel as though society is watching and reacting to our every move, keeping us stagnating in what we feel is safe. Passion does not come from comfort; it comes from pushing our limits.

Sometimes, our bliss is in the tiny things, but we shy away from reflecting into ourselves to find this joy or even to uncover the causes of our pain. Often, inner reflection comes into conflict with outer projection. Outer projection is what matters the most nowadays, especially for young people. They will focus their energy on what they are projecting out to the world, regardless of how they are suffering on the inside.

Here's an example. A young man gets a position in a company where he is making more money than his peers. He posts updates about how happy he is with his job. He shares photos of new restaurants he is trying, his new sports car, the exotic travels he has made. He gets comments from his friends about how envious they are and about how lucky he is. His parents tell him they are proud. Really, on the inside, this man feels as though he is living a life that is hollow, joyless, and shallow. He wants to do something more meaningful. He is passionate about helping people with disabilities but knows that his decision to pursue a career path where he will get paid significantly less will raise eyebrows. He has devoted a lot of time and money into a STEM career and is afraid of making a change. His parents borrowed money for his student loans, so he feels guilty that he is not happy.

Consequently, he becomes depressed and tries to soothe himself by focusing on the external validation he is receiving. He buys more things and takes more photos to help himself feel better. He will not ask for help because people will judge him. Twisted, right?

When you take the time to nurture your inner self, you can find your inner bliss. You can find your happiness. It is not by accident that we're in this universe. I think the world would be in a much better place if people started doing self-evaluation and reflection and concentrated on the inner self more, rather than chasing the outer projection.

Because the moment you start to listen to yourself, you can start to shut out all the noise.

Only then will you start finding perfection in imperfections. Tranquility in noise and chaos. And pure happiness in the small things in life.

When you find your bliss, you'll find new energy and

motivation to try new things, and doors will open for you where there were only walls.

While bliss doesn't insulate you from "life happens" situations, it allows you to reframe and see everything in a way that enables you to return quickly to a place of love, joy, and peace. Ultimately, you'll be able to have gratitude and find purpose in the highs and lows, the struggles and successes, the big and small, and through the simple and complex situations in life. When you attain your bliss, you are reborn.

FIND YOUR PASSION AND START LIVING A FULFILLING, BLISSFUL LIFE

Do you enjoy what you do? Do you know your passion?

Are you happy with the life you're leading today?

Like you, I was lost and struggled to find answers until I dived in and set myself on a journey to finding my passion and bliss. I have been slowly discovering the things I love to do and have remained committed to doing them.

I could go on and on about my story, but I want you to have your own, to find your life's purpose, passion, and bliss. I want you to wake up excited each day because you're doing something different. You are doing something that fills you up and gets you out of your head.

Finding your purpose, passion, and bliss in life is different for everyone. It is a personal journey. It is vital that you discover what you can do and who you are. It also is imperative that you focus on working towards a better, happier, healthier, and more blissful lifestyle. Start putting everything into action.

Sometimes, taking action to discover and practice what brings you joy is not easy. It takes persistence and dedication to find your passion and to reach your bliss. It takes time, energy, and openness to new things. Sometimes, it might require you to become vulnerable and take the path less traveled.

But the good thing is that, when following your passion and working towards attaining your bliss, you'll love every step, even when things get tough. You'll find amazing stuff, brilliant people, and exciting opportunities along the way. It is an awesome feeling to have!

Start today. Repeat simple habits that you find fulfilling. It could be hitting the gym, or taking a new music lesson, or learning something new, or helping in the community, or volunteering. Find those things that excite you to the core and create reasons to do them often. You will gradually have revealed parts of your purpose. Whatever it is, find something that you love and enjoy doing, and do it.

*One day you could be the one reflecting
on your life's journey and sharing how
you overcame your mountain of
doubts and insecurities.*

YOUR KEY TO SUCCESS

Throughout the past six chapters, you have heard a lot about my story and how I was able to discover my passion and bliss. I have also asked you a number of questions that can help you along the path to finding your passion and bliss. Remember, passion and bliss are entirely individual. One person might find their passion crunching numbers for a polling agency (such as Gallup or Quinnipiac), while another may discover theirs in doing the actual polling. Some may find their bliss in a corner office, and others in the great outdoors. It's all completely personal.

To help you on your way, I have developed this workbook. I have already given you things to think about; now I'm going to help you dig deep into your thought process to help you find out exactly who you are, as well as who you want to become. The pages ahead are the first concrete steps towards finding your passion. Take your time, think things through. Getting to know yourself will unlock your potential. Picture this: The book you have just read is the door. The workbook to follow is the lock, and your honest answers are the key to finding your passion and knowing your true potential. Get ready to start an incredible journey of self-discovery!

YOUR PASSION & PURPOSE WORKBOOK

*This is **your workbook and an intuitive tool to help you discover your passion and purpose**. The questions in the following sections are the same questions I asked myself when I was in pursuit of my calling.*

Now it's your turn to unlock your potential and begin living a more fulfilled life!

The best way to use this workbook is to take your time to reflect and answer questions thoughtfully, to discover more about where you have been, what parts of your life bring you the greatest happiness, and what you'd like to discover next on your journey to a more joyful and fulfilled life.

There are four sections to inspire you in this workbook.

- **Know Your Why**
- **Passion Is Not Something You Stumble Upon**
- **Clarifying Your Purpose**
- **Taking Inspired & Intentional Action**

Perhaps you are like me, and you will find that it is not just one thing that fulfills you, but it is many things that excite and ignite your soul.

KNOW YOUR WHY

You've taken the first step and just made one of the most intelligent investments in yourself and your personal growth. I applaud you, as will the world because the world needs passionate people now more than ever—people filled with intentional purpose and joy; who are ready, willing, and able to help us all become better together.

This workbook is a part of the "**It's Time to Start Living with Passion!**" community, book series, and online course program, and it will help you begin to understand where you are in life, as well as the strategies and tools you will need to embark on the journey of your dreams.

It's a practical, hands-on guide for discovering your purpose in this world and living the life you were made to live.

But before you begin, let's talk about the most important question you can ever ask yourself, and that question is **Why?**

Yes, I said, **"Why?"**

Ask yourself, "*Why* have I decided to embark on this journey to live a more passionate and purposeful life?"

Why? Because this simple one-word question will unlock the door to leveling up your life.

WHEN YOUR *WHY* IS CLEAR, YOUR *HOW* IS EASY.

Quick question: *When is the last time you truly focused on what you want out of life and why you want it?* Something tells me it has been a long time.

Getting clear about your desires and your goals and, more importantly, the reason you want them so badly will set you on a course to live your best life.

We will begin this together by identifying your unique blend of **gifts, talents, skills, opportunities,** and **dreams** in the following pages.

Remember, if at any time you feel like you need to reach out, you can do so by emailing me at info@jeanpaulpaulynice.com.

PASSION IS NOT SOMETHING YOU STUMBLE UPON

Passion is not something you stumble upon one day, or an idea that drops into your head while you are meditating, praying, or journaling. No, it is the exact opposite. Your passion will be revealed when you are in the process of discovering and experimenting with career options, hobbies, and interests.

You see, long before I launched my own company, I had tried my hand at a hundred-and-one-things. My first corporate job was in biotech, and while I enjoyed my undergraduate studies in biochemistry and molecular biology, I found my day-to-day responsibilities at work to be lonely, restrictive and suffocating. After quitting, I decided to try many different ways of living my life. It was by doing, trying, and deciding what resonated with me that I discovered the passion I was seeking.

If you approach it this way, uncovering your passion and purpose will be the biggest adventure of your life.

1. WHAT WOULD YOU COMFORTABLY DO IF YOU KNEW YOU COULD NOT FAIL?

Sometimes we don't take the risk, because we fear we might not make the goal. That is completely normal, but your path lies through the obstacle. If you truly want something, nothing will stop you.

2. HOW HAS YOUR PASSION CHANGED?

From your earliest memories, map out how your career, hobbies, and interests have changed over time. Do you remember why you made these choices? As you can see, you have already started down a path of discovery – let's do it with purpose.

CLARIFYING YOUR PURPOSE

You are so fortunate and blessed to have come to a point in your life where you want to transform yourself.

Most people ignore the nagging feeling that they could be doing so much more. Life is complicated, and it is challenging to keep up with everything going on—all the responsibilities, the obligations to others, even the crazy distractions. I'm sure there have been times when you have looked in the mirror and struggled to recognize yourself. *"Where did I go?"* you might have asked, wondered how you ended up where you are.

The reflective questions below will help you remember and get you back on the right track. The act of self-reflection is deep, and you must be honest and candid about your behaviors and beliefs which necessitates the process of asking yourself thought-provoking questions so that you can develop a deeper level of self-awareness. Again, take your time answering them and be as thoughtful and optimistically realistic as you can be.

1. WHO ARE YOU?

You are more than your name, your status, your current situation, or your career. What are some of your key personality traits? What is most important to you in life? What are your strengths? What are your weaknesses? Your values? What are you most grateful for?

2. WHAT DO YOU LOVE TO DO?

You may have forgotten, but I promise, if you reflect enough, you will remember. What makes you come alive? What excites you to the core? What are you most proud of? Whether at home or at work, what do you take the most pleasure in doing? What do you find yourself doing in your spare time? What do you get "lost" doing? What are you doing when time just seems to fly by? Who are you doing this for? Yourself? Others?

3. WHO DO YOU DO IT FOR?

Dig a little deeper. Think about the people you love to help. It could be members of your congregation or your yoga practice. Perhaps it is the students you teach, or your patients. It could be your brother, sister, father, wife, husband, or children. Think about the times you did the thing you love for another person, regardless of the circumstance. Who do you really connect with, and why?

4. WHAT DO THOSE PEOPLE WANT OR NEED?

What do the people that you love to help want or need from you? What do they come to you for? What are people always asking of you? Is it advice? Is it something you do really well?

5. HOW DO PEOPLE CHANGE OR TRANSFORM AS A RESULT OF WHAT YOU DO FOR THEM?

When you give these people what they need or want, who do they become? How do you help them become better versions of who they are?

6. HAVE YOU ACHIEVED WHAT YOU WANTED TO ACHIEVE THIS YEAR? IF NO, WHY NOT?

Be careful not to fall into a victim mindset here; believe me, it is easy to do. Think about all of the promises you haven't kept to yourself. How many times have you put off doing something for yourself because of lack of time or energy?

7. ARE YOU PUTTING IN THE WORK, THE SWEAT, AND THE TIME TO DISCOVER YOUR PASSION AND LIVE A LIFE OF FULFILLMENT?

When was the last time you really thought about yourself and what you really want? Perhaps you are working on your goals right now. Think about what is missing. What would be the one thing you could do that could add more excitement to your future?

8. WHAT WOULD YOU DO WITHOUT EXPECTING A PAYCHECK?

This could be anything, so let your imagination run wild. Maybe you love to make people laugh, or you secretly want to write lyrics. Perhaps bike tours through the Tuscan countryside would be something you would gladly do without getting paid because you enjoy it so much yourself. Go ahead, dream away.

9. WHAT WOULD YOUR PROFESSIONAL LIFE BE LIKE? WHAT WOULD YOU BE DOING TO MAKE A LIVING?

This is a big one, because most of us still have to make a living to make ends meet, so you might as well be doing something you really enjoy. Now, here is where you must be a bit more optimistically realistic. You must keep your budget in mind as you transition, but remember, where there is a will, there is a way.

10. WHAT COULD YOU BE DOING WITH YOUR FREE TIME?

Time spent passively watching Netflix could be time spent actively pursuing your passion. What could you be doing instead? Think about how you could add passion to your free time as you design a life you love.

11. WOULD YOU BE HELPING OTHERS? IF SO, WHAT WOULD YOU BE DOING TO HELP THEM?

Most neuroscientists know that healthy relationships lead to longevity and an improvement in the quality of our lives. You have unique talents that could be shared with the world. Perhaps it is teaching tech to seniors, or volunteering to help protect your neighborhood. Think about your skills, talents, and interests, and how they might help others.

12. WHAT KIND OF RELATIONSHIP WOULD YOU HAVE WITH YOURSELF?

This is also a big one. You are your own best friend, and understanding your self-worth and how you want to be treated is the start of a life filled with passion and purpose.

TAKING INSPIRED & INTENTIONAL ACTION

This part is the "doing part" that I referred to in the **Passion is Not Something You Stumble Upon** section of the workbook. The part where you get to choose what you would like to try next in your life—the new habits you will experiment with, the interesting books you will read, foods you will discover, classes you will take, and health and wellness programs you will try.

Some of the first habits I recommend to my clients start with the basics:

- Make rest a priority. Get a good night's sleep.
- Take a walk. Exercise. Engage your body. Jim Kwik, an optimal brain performance expert, says, "*The mind grooves when the body moves.*"
- Develop the habit of getting up earlier. Create a morning mantra, meditation, and visualization.
- Eat healthy food. Our body and mind are the products of what we eat.

If you have decided that you want to learn how to dance, then book your first lesson today. Perhaps you want to learn how to trade stocks, or maybe learn how to cook plant-based meals or invest in Bitcoin. Whatever your interests are, do not delay!

The most important part is that you have fun and remember . . .

This is *your* journey. Enjoy each and every step of the way.

About Jean Paul Paulynice: In His Own Words

I am Jean Paul Paulynice, a business strategist, motivational coach, and visionary author. I am also the Founder and Executive Director of Paulynice Consulting Group, a professional business consulting firm for small businesses and start-ups. I have championed individuals and business owners while helping them become unstoppable in all areas of their lives.

I hold an MBA with dual concentrations in Finance and Management Information Systems from Clark University. I also hold an undergraduate degree with dual concentrations in Biochemistry and Molecular Biology from the University of Massachusetts, Amherst.

I am not someone who is defined by my books or an impressive background. I am a soul, *driven by a passion* for helping people realize their full potential, be it in business or their personal lives. As a firm believer in empowerment and self-development, I have chosen a path less traveled — one that leads me to care for the people with whom I work. The vast knowledge I have gained from the corporate world has helped me guide small business owners to grow and protect their endeavors, so they become highly successful entities.

My business model is simple. I give my clients the upper hand in an industry that is sometimes not so kind to them. I do this, at a fraction of the price of the competition, because as a fellow small business owner, I know how difficult it is to remain competitive and profitable. Every client I serve gives me the honor of being part of their success story, and the joy that comes with it is priceless.

I desire to see people conquer their fears, follow their passions, and reach their full potential. I strive to do this in every way I can, including writing and developing materials that further this cause.

I was born in Haiti and am a loving husband, a caring father of two. When I am not providing consultancy services for businesses or writing, I enjoy spending time with my family.

Please visit my professional website if you'd like my help in achieving your goals:

https://www.paulyniceconsulting.com

To learn more about me and read my other books, please visit

https://www.jeanpaulpaulynice.com.

Join me on Social Media

https://www.facebook.com/jeanpaulpaulynice/
https://twitter.com/paulynice
https://www.linkedin.com/in/jnplnce/
https://www.instagram.com/jeanpaulpaulynice/

Notes

Notes

Notes

CPSIA information can be obtained
at www.ICGtesting.com
Printed in the USA
LVHW100638261119
638523LV00004B/284/P

9 781733 042796